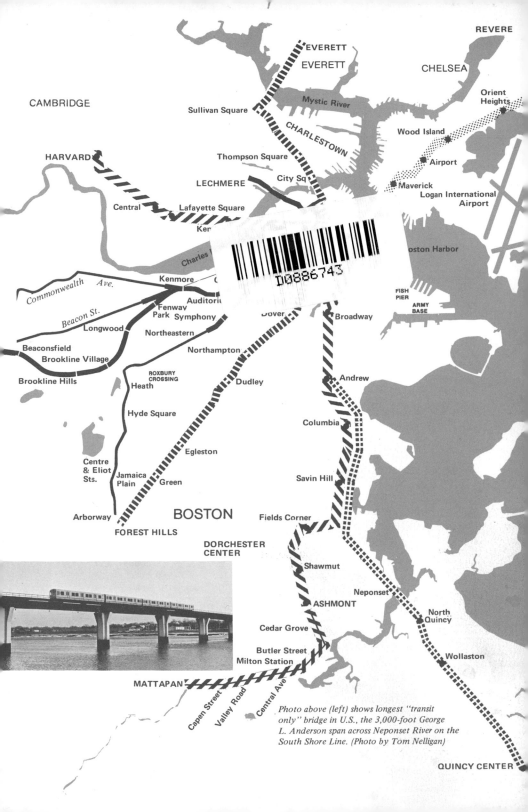

REVERE

EVERETT
EVERETT

CHELSEA

CAMBRIDGE

Mystic River

Orient
Heights

Sullivan Square

Wood Island

CHARLESTOWN

HARVARD

Airport

Thompson Square

Maverick

Central

LECHMERE
Lafayette Square

City Sq

Logan International
Airport

Ker

Charles

oston Harbor

Kenmore

FISH
PIER

ARMY
BASE

Commonwealth   Ave.

Auditori

Beacon St.

Fenway
Park   Symphony

Dover

Broadway

Longwood

Northeastern

Beaconsfield
Brookline Village

Northampton

Andrew

Brookline Hills

ROXBURY
CROSSING
Heath

Dudley

Columbia

Hyde Square

Savin Hill

Egleston

Centre
& Eliot
Sts.

Jamaica
Plain   Green

Fields Corner

Arborway

BOSTON

FOREST HILLS

DORCHESTER
CENTER

Shawmut

Neponset

ASHMONT

North
Quincy

Cedar Grove

Butler Street
Milton Station

Wollaston

MATTAPAN

Capen Street   Valley Road   Central Ave.

Photo above (left) shows longest "transit only" bridge in U.S., the 3,000-foot George L. Anderson span across Neponset River on the South Shore Line. (Photo by Tom Nelligan)

QUINCY CENTER

CHANGE AT PARK STREET UNDER

Park Street Under . . . and here a four-car train of 01400 series cars—Pullman-Standard products, class of 1963—heads for Harvard Square. (Tom Nelligan photo)

BRIAN J. CUDAHY

CHANGE AT
PARK STREET UNDER

The Story of Boston's Subways

THE STEPHEN GREENE PRESS * * * **BRATTLEBORO, VERMONT**

This book has been manufactured in the United States of America: designed by Russel Hamilton, printed by The Vermont Printing Company and bound by The Book Press. It is published by The Stephen Greene Press, Brattleboro, Vermont 05301. Library of Congress catalog card number: 72-81531. ISBN: 0-8289-0173-2

PREFACE

In 1946, in the Introduction and text for the book *Dahl's Boston,* the then Associate Editor of *Atlantic Monthly,* Charles W. Morton, wrote:

"Metropolitan Boston is a collection of cities and towns, each fiercely autonomous . . . holding in all some two million residents in a wide strip along the shores of Massachusetts Bay. In any other part of the United States, all these would have been merged long since into a single city.

"The mainstay of Boston transportation facilities is a thing called the Boston Elevated Railway or 'the El.' It is hardly a precise title for the assortment of busses, streetcars, trackless trolleys, and subways which make up the system. The trolleys run below ground and up in the air as well as at street level. The subway is the oldest in the United States, as none of its passengers could doubt."

The intervening twenty-five years have seen some changes made, both in quantity and quality. The El as a corporate entity is gone. Instead, there is the M.B.T.A.—Massachusetts Bay Transportation Authority—which operates its conglomerate of lines radiating into the now even more populated half-wheel of territory whose circumference is Route 128.

Withal, the veritable axle of "the Hub" is still the angle of Boston Common where Park Street slants downward from the State House into Tremont. Just under the sidewalks is the original terminal of the original Boston subway. This book marks the 75th Anniversary of its construction and operation.

ACKNOWLEDGEMENTS

SPECIAL THANKS are in order to the several libraries whose facilities were used in the preparation of this book. The Boston Public Library at Copley Square was especially cooperative and helpful, as was Bapst Memorial Library at Boston College. Many valuable papers and documents were provided by the Planning Library of the Massachusetts Bay Transportation Authority. Permission to quote Charles W. Morton, above, was granted by his widow, Mrs. Mildred Sylvester.

Professor John Power, of Boston College, read the manuscript and shared recollections of the Boston El. Mr. George Sanborn of the M.B.T.A. made available the historical photographs contained in the book, and Mr. Thomas Nelligan's skill with camera and enlarger is responsible for many of the contemporary photographs in the pages that follow. Finally Mr. Russel Hamilton, of The Stephen Greene Press, must be thanked for his patience in seeing the manuscript through to publication.

Boston College. Chestnut Hill, Massachusetts. April 25, 1972

CHANGE AT PARK STREET UNDER

INTRODUCTION

THE TEMPERATURE was in the low 80s, the humidity a comfortable 45. Over Boston Harbor puffy white clouds drifted through the clear sky of a perfect late summer afternoon. It was a day made to order for a ride in the country, a stroll through the park, fishing off a deserted wharf, or—opening a new subway line. The date: Wednesday, September 1, 1971.

Onward from two o'clock invited guests began to arrive at the Eliot Shops of the Massachusetts Bay Transportation Authority in Cambridge, adjacent to the venerable brick buildings of Harvard University. Each, after displaying a pre-issued and color-coded name tag, was escorted aboard one of three flag-draped aluminum subway trains. A few minutes after three, the first official train, made up of four 69-foot "brushed aluminum" cars, slid out of Track Three inside the machine shop, ducked into a tunnel portal at the north end of the yard, and headed for Quincy Center.

The route used by all three ceremonial trains followed an older subway line from Cambridge to South Boston; thereafter a newly constructed $75.4 million, 6.25-mile transit extension that was once the right-of-way of the Old Colony Line of the New York, New Haven and Hartford Railroad. In July of 1959 the financially troubled New Haven had abandoned passenger service to Old Colony points; M.B.T.A. broke ground for its transit project in August, 1966, after several years of negotiation. The initial test trains to run over any portion of the new transit route did so in May, 1971, and by mid-summer the test runs extended all the way to Quincy Center.

The very latest in transit hardware can be found on the line, including automatic in-cab signaling and train control, welded rail mounted on concrete ties, and two-way radio communication between trains and the line's dispatcher. A striking 3000-foot arch bridge, named in honor of former M.B.T.A. director George L. Anderson, carries trains over the Neponset River. Three new stations in suburban Norfolk County are distinctive, functional, modern, and have large "park 'n ride" auto lots. Another 3.2 miles to Braintree are planned for the near future.

The rolling stock—24 single-unit cars, 01500 series, and 26 pairs of two-car units (*i.e.* 52 cars) in the 01600 series—have been described by the trade publication *Railway Age* as "a proper blending of rider appeal with earthy practicality." And that's a fair assessment. Built by Pullman-Standard at a cost of $12.8 million, they are powered by four 100 hp Westinghouse "Tracpak" motors per car. Acceleration from dead stop is at 2.5 mphps; top speed is 70 mph. Normal stopping is by dynamic brake down to 15 mph, when an air system cuts in to bring the train to a full stop.

The units are air-conditioned, but despite this and other sophisticated hardware, gross weight is low—only 64,000 pounds for each single-unit 01500, while the 01600s weigh but 61,000. By contrast, New York operates a fleet of comparable stainless steel cars which are nine feet shorter but weigh 68,500 pounds each. Extensive use of aluminum in the M.B.T.A. car helps make for the lesser tonnage.

At Quincy Center formal dedication ceremonies took place in the plaza outside the station entrance as soon as the three specials

Train of 01500 and 01600 class cars at South Station Under. (Nelligan)

Sept. 1, 1971, and the first official train to run over the new South Shore Line prepares to leave Eliot shops. (Author photo) At right, in conductor's hat, the "T"'s Gen. Mgr., Joseph C. Kelly, distributes souvenir tokens to invited guests on the inaugural run. (Photo from M.B.T.A.)

arrived. Secretary of Transportation John Volpe, himself a former Massachusetts governor, the M.B.T.A.'s very popular General Manager, Joseph C. Kelly, and other officials took to the podium proclaiming that a new day was dawning for Boston transportation. A new day literally dawned less than fourteen hours later at 5:24 A.M. when regular revenue service began out of Quincy Center. By the end of the month the new line was carrying some 20,000 daily riders, a number which cautious M.B.T.A. officials had predicted would not be achieved until after a full year of operation.

Important as is the new Quincy extension in the M.B.T.A.'s scheme of things, its opening may not, in retrospect, have been the most significant transit event of 1971. Massachusetts Governor Francis Sargent—who himself handled the inaugural controls for a short distance on the very first September 1st South Shore opening special—affixed his signature on November 12th to the bottom of a four-page document disarmingly entitled "Chapter 1075." In "legalese," this was described as "an act relative to the administration and operation of the Massachusetts Bay Transportation Authority, and increasing the amount of bonds which may be issued by said authority." This legislation empowered the M.B.T.A. to sell an additional $124 million in bonds which, coupled with two-thirds matching Federal funds as provided by the 1970 Urban Mass Transportation Assistance Act, will enable the authority to outdo its own past performance in improvement and expansion.

M.B.T.A. was created by the Massachusetts legislature in 1964, at which time it was given authority to float some $225 million for capital projects. The Quincy Line, as an instance, was built with these funds plus matching Federal dollars. But the 1964 money was either spent or committed by 1971—thus it was important that the M.B.T.A.'s request for more funds be approved. It was a very close roll-call vote in both houses, where the transit authority has more than its fair share of legislator-critics. (A similar petition had been defeated in 1970.) But at last the money was available, and now the "T" could turn its attention to a variety of projects that will still further improve the quality and availability of transit in the Boston metropolitan area.

But this all speaks to the future. In point of fact the M.B.T.A. is also heir to a solid, if occasionally odd-ball, tradition that goes back to the last decade of the 19th century, and which embraces some colorful and interesting developments in the years of the present century as well—our story for the pages to come.

7

The original Public Gardens incline of the 1897 Boston trolley subway. This incline was replaced by a new and different ramp at the same location (see map below) in 1914. The proposed "back alley" route between Tremont and Washington Streets is approximated on the map by dotted line ----------------

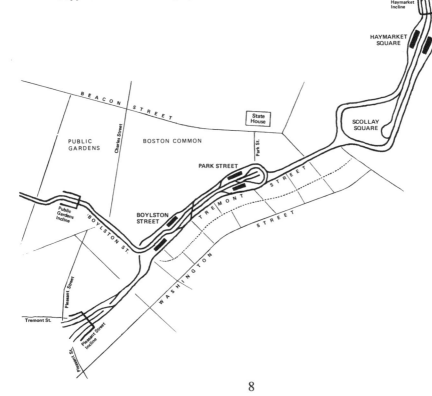

1. SEPTEMBER 1, 1897

BOSTON STOLE A MARCH on the entire nation when it opened America's very first subway in the waning years of the 19th century. Before this unprecedented event could come to pass, several preliminary scenarios had first to be acted out. Not the least was that the basic hardware necessary to build and operate a subway had to be invented!

An experimental installation at the Berlin Industrial Exposition in 1879 is generally regarded as the first successful carriage of passengers by electric-powered vehicles. The overseer of this technological breakthrough was a gentleman named Werner Siemens. Following his lead, others worked at perfecting the new technology by ironing out various kinks. Things moved swiftly; early in 1888 the city of Richmond, Virginia, boasted that *its* entire fleet of horse-drawn street cars had been equipped with electric motors. This was the first successful deployment of the new energy source on a large scale.

A Connecticut-born Annapolis graduate named Frank Sprague was the out-and-out genius who did more than any score of people in the field. He not only managed the Richmond installation; his later invention of the system called "multiple-unit control" ranks in significance only slightly below the wheel itself in the history of transportation. (The multiple-unit control enabled a single operator to control a multi-car train from the leading car, the head end. More on this later.)

Measured against today's space-age standards, Sprague's work may seem crude and unimpressive; but the technical and engineering difficulties he faced were genuine and real in the 1880s. His success in overcoming them should not be discounted.

During the summer of '88, the president of one of the largest horse-car companies in the country traveled south to inspect

Sprague's work at Richmond. His name was Henry H. Whitney, and the firm he headed up was Boston's West End Street Railway. In the previous year, 1887, the Massachusetts legislature enacted a bill bringing the West End company into existence, essentially a sensible merger of separate and competing firms. Among the first business Whitney felt obliged to deal with was conversion of the company's horse-cars to efficient and reliable mechanical power. But which form? Cable cars? Though already popular in some cities, these were *very* expensive and, furthermore, might prove impractical on the narrow, twisting streets of Boston, "the Hub." And so Whitney journeyed to Richmond, willing to be influenced by what he might find there.

Serious doubts plagued him at first. In the peaceful, almost rural precincts of the quiet Southern city electric trolleys performed their routines with leisurely ease. Would such prove practical in brisk, congested Boston? Could, say, a large number of cars be started all at once? Would the slim overhead wire safely carry the electrical load needed?

Sprague, responding to Whitney's reservations, decided to find out. As the cars completed their runs one summer's day in that year of '88, they were brought together at one end of the line. Power from the generating station was maintained at peak levels so that shortly after midnight, at a lantern signal from Sprague, 22 cars "juiced up" simultaneously. No motors melted, no fuses "blew," Whitney was convinced—and Sprague got a contract for the electrification of Boston's West End lines. In January of '89 the Hub boasted its first trolley cars—and so popular did they become that Oliver Wendell Holmes took note with these lines:

> *Since then on many a car you'll see*
> *A broomstick plain as plain can be;*
> *On every stick there's a witch astride—*
> *The string you see to her leg is tied.*

Still, even electric power fortified by Holmes' verse proved insufficient to allay Boston's transportation woes. Narrow streets in the business district were simply incapable of providing sufficient clearance for all the cars ferrying passengers downtown. Tremont Street saw trolleys lined up "bumper to bumper," in today's phrase, whereat civic leaders—in due course—urged amelioration of the electromotive congestion.

In 1892 a state commission prepared a comprehensive analysis detailing the extent of the problem, also calling for a network of elevated railways plus an underground tunnel, of all things, so that West End trolley cars would both be removed from city streets and provide more efficient service in downtown areas. For its time, this was a breathtaking proposal, not likely to win quick, much less universal, approval by Bostonians. West End management itself did not at all welcome the prospect of a subway—especially with the kind of lease arrangement the legislature seemed bent on enacting. The company was not alone. Certain old-line residents viewed the notion of a subway with slightly less alarm, say, than a report of Attila the Hun marching east through Dedham. Some downtown property owners were convinced that their Tremont Street buildings would be undermined by the construction, and eventually collapse. But by far the most emotional response was generated by the thought of hordes of common laborers digging up sacred Boston Common. "And they dare to call this progress?" one be-whiskered Beacon Hill gentleman remarked to his luncheon associates as he squeezed a lemon wedge over his broiled scrod at the Parker House.

Further negativism of undetermined proportion was the feeling, reflected in the newspapers, that many potential passengers would be uneasy about riding through tunnels below ground, a Stygian territory generally associated with such unsavory things as sewers and gas mains and the less sociable members of the rodent and reptile families.

In July, 1894, the General Court—to give the Massachusetts legislature its proper name, then and now—did enact a bill which authorized incorporation of a firm called the Boston Elevated Railway Company, also the formation of a public agency, the Boston Transit Commission. The commission was to make final determination of the proper solution to the area's transit problems and, furthermore, to see its plan through to fruition. Precisely what the Boston Elevated Railway was all about will emerge hereafter.

This legislation passed in the final days of the General Court's 1894 session, a style of last-minute statecraft many Bostonians regarded as at least suspicious and, very likely, devious. One disconsolate Back Bay resident, a staunch believer in the *status quo,* remarked that "they only got away with this because the important people were all vacationing when the bill was voted."

The non-absentee "they" were, of course, the "barbarians" who championed so iconoclastic a notion as a downtown subway; but

11

THE propaganda picture! (M.B.T.A.)

"they" were vindicated when the people of Boston accepted the legislation by referendum. The final tally was close, very close—15,369 to 14,298. There followed attempts to stop the subway *via* the courts. All were unsuccessful.

When the Transit Commission got to work several possibilities were reviewed—one of them the transit concept already applied in New York, Chicago and Brooklyn—an elevated railway. When double-printed photographs were prepared, dubbing in an "el" structure complete with a train rumbling over Tremont Street past Park Street Church, the idea earned swift oblivion. Eventually, Boston would build elevated lines, but *never* in the central business district of the city adjacent to the Common and the Public Gardens.

One plan, seriously considered, proposed a surface-level "alley" between and parallel to Tremont and Washington Streets (see map). Its chief flaw was operational—too many grade crossings! On top of that, it would have required extensive land-taking in an area where real estate was extremely valuable.

Thus Boston veered to the "European transit system," as one newspaper put it—surely a valid description, since London, Glasgow and Paris all had operating subway systems at the time. The world's very first subway, London's, dated from the mid-Victorian month of January, 1863, when steam-powered trains began hauling the Queen's subjects the three and three-fourths miles between Farringdon and Paddington. (In America, the battles of Gettysburg and Vicksburg were yet to be fought!)

The Boston project, headed up by Chief Engineer Howard A. Carsen, called for a subway tunnel for trolley cars that would lead into central downtown from three directions, two from the south and one from the north. The northern "incline"—the term for a subway entry ramp—was located beyond Haymarket Square; it led up to the North Union Station. One of the southern inclines was along Boylston Street at the Public Gardens; the other was at Tremont and Broadway, called Pleasant Street in 1897. It was planned that cars could run through the subway from one end to the other; in addition three underground loops would enable trolleys to reverse direction inside the subway, returning to their point of origin. Its length? "The tunnel will comprehend a distance of two and two-thirds miles."

European engineers had perfected two noteworthy styles of subway construction. London pioneered the deep underground "tube," constructed by tunneling without disruption of surface traffic, although this had not been used for the original Farringdon-Paddington line. The tunnel was pieced together within the bore with "iron segmental linings," forming a secure and even watertight structure. ·

Car No. 2512 is typical of the kind of trolleys the West End Street Railway used when Boston opened the first subway on the American continent in 1897. (M.B.T.A.)

Paris, on the other hand, had gone in for extensive use of masonry arches in subway construction. The tunnel was located immediately below ground level, requiring surface excavation for the length of the route. But the Paris method had a serious drawback: the tunnel was not a self-contained structure, and thus would not tolerate underground disruption adjacent to it. Therefore, in Boston, a hybrid concept evolved: to build a steel and concrete tunnel chiefly in open excavation, like Paris, but "independent of lateral ground support, in the sense that it can stand by itself, if earth is removed from about it," as *Scientific American* reported. This technique soon after became standard practice in nearly all American subway construction, although London-style deep tunnel construction would be used from time to time in Boston as well as other U.S. cities, but only when surface excavation was not feasible.

During construction, efforts were made to insure as normal a flow of surface traffic as could be managed; indeed it was legally stipulated that during daylight hours Tremont Street had to be available for regular use. So, much work had to be done at night.

On March 28, 1895, ground was broken for the new subway in the Public Gardens opposite the Providence Railway depot close to Boylston Street, thus launching a three-year project. Many unexpected problems cropped up, such as incorrect and even nonexisting maps supposedly giving precise locations of sewer, water and gas lines. Beds of quicksand gave trouble; an explosion in the excavation at Boylston and Tremont Streets killed nine. A further macabre duty was the reinterment of the remains of 910 bodies exhumed as the excavators worked their way through colonial burial grounds.

Ventilation was a matter of serious concern to the early subway builders. Their concern may seem exaggerated to us today, but it should be remembered that at the turn of the century pulmonary disease was man's most dreaded killer, so that worry about the quality of air in the tunnels was a manifestation of the human survival instinct. After the Boston subway opened, most granted it very high marks. Ventilation shafts at several points along the route provided air of a quality much better than London's, for example, as rated by no less an authority than *The New York Times*. Survival, too, expressed itself in worry about the temperature of the tunnels; the commission was fearful that the subway would be *too cool* during the hot days of summer, and actually

14

made efforts to heat the stations. The assumption was that it was unnatural and injurious to have the subway more than a few degrees different from the outside temperature.

The subway cost $5 million. The initial leg was ready for service in the autumn of 1897, connecting Park Street terminal with the Boylston-Public Gardens incline. It received uniformly, if not universally, favorable comment.

"The air is good, the temperature is comfortable, and the light-hued walls reflect the glow of many hundreds of incandescent lamps that brightly illuminate it," one magazine noted. *The Boston Journal* modestly proclaimed that "our park system, our union stations, and now our subway have opened the eyes of the country to the fact that this city is more than a centre of literary and historic associations, and that it has an eye on the future as well as to the past." Among those whose eyes were definitely opened was *The New York Times:* "That so conservative an American town should happen to be the pioneer in adopting this is viewed as remarkable."

The subway entrances drew comment. Because much care had gone into their "kiosk" design, it was frustrating for the Transit Commission to hear them described as "resembling mausoleums." (A year later when the subway was opened between Park Street and the Haymarket incline, the Scollay Square kiosk was characterized as "pretentiously monumental . . . unnecessary and in bad taste.") On the question of the artistic merits of the subway generally, *Harper's Weekly* felt that the work's "engineering character . . . is too boldly manifest, and the architectural opportunities have not been sufficiently improved."

The kiosk at Adams Square was quite elaborate. Indeed, some architects felt it was so ornate as to be in bad taste! It was replaced later by a more conventional kiosk. In 1963, as part of Boston's Government Center renewal project, the subway was slightly rerouted and the Adams Square stop eliminated. (M.B.T.A.)

15

Then came opening day itself! Early on the morning of Wednesday, September 1, 1897, four-wheel, open-bench car No. 1752 moved out of the Allston car barns, in the presence of crowds gathered at the depot in tribute to this extraordinary event. Conductor Gilman T. Trufant and motorman James Reed, two West End veterans, were to pilot No. 1752 into the new Tremont Street subway. If they kept to their schedule, they would get to the incline ahead of a Cypress Street car from Brookline and thus would be the immortal first trolley to carry revenue passengers into the new facility.

Trufant admitted he had slept little in nervous anticipation of the event, and as soon as Reed intoned "All aboard for the subway and Park Street," things were under way. The motorman "compelled the pent-up lightning to do his bidding"—the language is *The Boston Globe*'s—and "the trolley hissed along like a brood of vipers." Suspense mounted as No. 1752 was delayed on its intown run and started to fall minutes behind its schedule; surely the Cypress Street rival would get to the subway first? It did not. As No. 1752 passed the intersection of Boylston and Huntington, with no competition in sight, its destiny was assured. At 6:01 A.M., a huge throng lining both sides of the ramp, the car swung off Boylston Street into the incline; three minutes later it was abreast the platform at Park Street. Boston had done it—had planned, built and this day opened the first subway in the new world!

Growth of residential communities in and around Boston was greatly assisted by the availability of convenient, reliable mass transportation, a process described and documented in the book "Streetcar Suburbs" by Sam B. Warner, Jr., published 1962 jointly by Harvard and M.I.T. Here's a photograph of the action—a trolley at Spring and Center Streets, West Roxbury, about to depart for a connection with the Main Line El, Feb. 29, 1904. Yes, it was leap year! (M.B.T.A.)

2. THE MAIN LINE EL

T HE MOST SIGNIFICANT RESULT of the new subway was: it did
precisely what it was supposed to do. It freed up the downtown streets. "The effect was like that when a barrier is removed
from the channel of a clogged-up river," as one contemporary ac-
count put it. Previously, 200 trolleys often plied Tremont Street
in each direction every hour, to hopeless confusion and the ruina-
tion of schedules. A month after the subway opened, it comfortably
took care of 282 cars per hour.

Flushed with the triumph of the Tremont Street operation, Boston moved ahead on the still grander transit plans already spelled
out by the original enabling legislation. Roxbury, East Boston,
Charlestown, Cambridge!

The 1897 subway drew on only two of three technological innovations then available for transit planners: electric power itself
and underground tunnels for the right-of-way. The third development was Frank Sprague's multiple-unit control, first put to use
on the South Side Elevated in Chicago, likewise in 1897. Boston's
next subway would make use of all three innovations.

This was to be a combination subway and elevated line from
the residential areas of Roxbury and Charlestown through the
heart of downtown Boston. Different also from the older line would
be trains of multiple-unit cars loading and unloading passengers
at floor-level platforms, a far more efficient procedure. And, instead of taking electrical current by trolley from overhead wire,
the new line would employ track-level, third-rail current collection.

The agency designated to build most of, and to operate all of
this route was the Boston Elevated Railway Company—a name
that would soon and often be abbreviated, in Boston parlance, to
"Boston El," "the Elevated," the "El Company" or a crisp "the
El." It was a corporation born of the same 1894 enabling legisla-

17

*It's Spring, 1901, just before the Main Line El opened for passenger
service, but trains are running up and down the line to familiarize crews
with the new equipment. Above, headed for Dudley, a two-car train
pauses at Northampton Street station. (Bradley H. Clarke collection)*

tion as the original subway. Legally, under the provisions of a 20-
year lease negotiated with the Transit Commission in 1896, and
for an annual rental amounting to 4⅞% of the subway's construction cost—plus five cents per trolley car using the facility—the
Tremont Street subway was the province of the West End Street
Railway. Nevertheless, there began within months of the subway's

*The station house at Thompson Square blends well into the Victorian architecture
in Charlestown. It's hard to tell that this photo was taken in 1972! (Nelligan)*

opening a series of complex legal moves that would culminate in BE Ry's complete takeover of the West End.

The idea of an elevated railway was scarcely new at this juncture. New York had opened its first "el" in 1870; by 1880 several steam-powered lines ran the length of Manhattan Island, which were, of course, eventually electrified. But this was a kind of "progress" that many Bostonians looked on as downright retrogressive, given the demonstrated practicability of a subway. However, els were much cheaper to build and that, really, was the nub of the matter. BE Ry tried to sweeten the pill by taking pains with the design of the station structures on the el—the company actually held a competition among architects before adopting a basic plan —but many saw it as "ludicrous in the extreme to complement our fine subway with a system of transit that is already out of favor in major cities." A later commentator spoke of the "hideous structures which the Boston elevated company has been allowed to disfigure and darken our streets with. . . ."

In early June, 1901, Col. William A. Gaston, Chairman of the Board of Directors of the Boston El, asked the state's Railroad Commissioners for authorization to open the company's new rapid transit line—given the route name of "Main Line El"—to public use. Permission granted; Monday, June 10th, was named as the target date for service to begin.

But official permission was by no means the final step in readying the route for service. Though elevated segments of the Sullivan Square-to-Dudley line were complete, the essential link-up with the four-year-old Tremont Street subway, through which the el trains would also operate, could not be completed until the last possible moment. Routing of el trains through the trolley subway would exclude "all of the surface cars which have been running thereon between Pleasant Street and the Causeway Street entrance at North Union Station," as one newspaper reported. In numerical terms 1,500 daily trolley trips would be eliminated from the subway, and no street cars at all would use the tunnels between Boylston and Pleasant as well as between Park Street and Scollay Square. Plans were made to effect the final changeover on the weekend of June 8th-10th.

At 8:15 P.M. on Saturday evening, June 8th, trolley car No. 2369 on the Franklin Park-Humbolt Avenue line emerged from the subway's Pleasant Street portal. Motorman Thomas McAvoy and Conductor Alexander Anderson had sixteen passengers in their charge; it would be the last trolley to use that incline for over seven years. The car had scarcely moved out into Pleasant Street when waiting crews set to work tearing up trackage and installing the final connecting rails to a ramp leading up to the elevated. Just outside the tunnel portal a wooden center-island platform would now serve as Pleasant Street station for m.u. (multiple-unit) trains.

In the tunnel itself, additional frantic activity was under way to meet the week-end deadline. Carpenters' hammers echoed from station to station as platforms were "superimposed over the regular platforms . . . to bring passengers on a level with the cars." These were placed alongside the subway's outside tracks on which the multiple-unit "elevated" trains would run.

The southbound track was pronounced ready at five o'clock Sunday morning, and at 7:00 A.M. BE Ry Superintendent S. S. Neff ran a test train over the entire line—Sullivan to Dudley. All that day "school trains" were sent up and down the line to acquaint operating employees with the route, even as tunnel track gangs were finishing off their assignments. The conversion was completed in time for the inaugural on Monday morning.

Late Sunday afternoon, a Col. Shepard, the Boston representative of the Sprague people, opined that "the people of Boston ought to feel proud of this road. There is nothing equal to it in the world. A train may be started and stopped at any grade with ease." One comparison stressed in discussions of the new el pointed out that a 90-ton, three-car train could call on 900 horsepower for tractive effort, whereas the 1000-ton consist of the New York Central Railroad's crack *Empire State Express* had but 1,000 hp at its disposal.

A massive change in surface car operations coincided with the opening of the new line. Chiefly, this involved routing cars that had previously gone all the way downtown into one or more of the new el terminals. Indeed, so complicated were the changes that BE Ry management quite seriously suggested that passengers pin copies of the new timetables inside their hats.

At Dudley (see diagram) two sets of street car tracks ran up a pair of ramps to el platform level for easy transfer. Each of these looped and returned to the street, so that several car lines could be accommodated on just two tracks. The loop track to the west of the el platform would be used by car lines into the growing areas of Forest Hills, Jamaica Plain and Roxbury Crossing. The loop

20

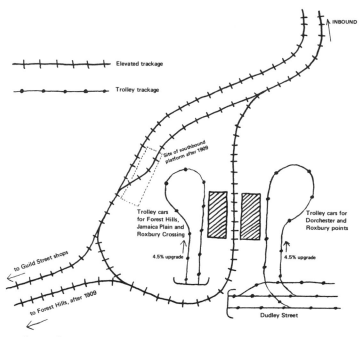

INBOUND

Elevated trackage

Trolley trackage

Site of southbound platform after 1909

Trolley cars for Forest Hills, Jamaica Plain and Roxbury Crossing

Trolley cars for Dorchester and Roxbury points

to Guild Street shops

4.5% upgrade

4.5% upgrade

to Forest Hills, after 1909

Dudley Street

track to the east would be used by a half-dozen or more lines that fanned out into Roxbury and Dorchester.

Under the high vault of the Sullivan Square train shed, 10 stub-end trolley tracks—five on either side of the single elevated track —provided terminal facilities for the many feeder street car lines connecting with the el at this point. All of these tracks entered the terminal shed on ramps located on the north side; only the el itself had access from the south. It should also be noted that when the Main Line El opened in 1901 both Sullivan Square and Dudley Street had only a single unloading point for el trains. Today each has separate—and separated—platforms for both northbound and southbound trains.

On that opening Monday morning, more people than could be accommodated were on hand to ride the first revenue trains. At 5:00 A.M. over 500 were at Dudley; one Charles Cutter of Worcester Place purchased the first ticket. As a good luck gesture, his nickel was returned.

Precisely at 5:25 A.M. wooden el cars Nos. 065, 056 and 082 left Dudley on the line's first run, a motorman named Dolan doing the head-end honors. But the train might have had a hex on it— near Boylston station the air brakes locked! Officials of the El spent fifteen feverish minutes correcting the trouble. The festive atmosphere in the train wasn't even slightly diminished by the mishap; one passenger cracked: "We're right under the Touraine; all out for breakfast."

At Sullivan there was confusion. The crowd gathered at street level even earlier than at Dudley. No record of who purchased the first ticket was possible, such was the press. Frustration, too, was felt when three trolleys rumbled up the ramp into the overhead train shed, where it was much easier for the transfer passengers to board the first el train than the hardy souls who had waited at street level in pre-dawn darkness. First trolley into the shed was from Medford, No. 2935; No. 2916 followed, also a Medford car; and No. 2949, out of Everett, was third.

Supt. Neff had come to Boston after a stint on the elevated lines of Chicago. Described now as a man "just as proud of the city as a native," he had made the final test run over the entire line at 4:00 A.M. on Monday. At 5:20 he ordered the first train into Sullivan station from the adjacent storage yard; by 5:28 it was full, and at 5:30 it departed, with Neff himself at the controls. Exactly 23½ minutes later the train reached Dudley.

Over 200,000 fares were paid on that first day, an extraordinary count compared to today's turnstile tally of about 150,000 daily on a much-expanded Main Line El. Speaking of turnstiles, incidentally, calls attention to the fact that in 1901 BE Ry did not use such hardware. The system then in force required passengers to purchase a ticket from what, today, would be the change booth and deposit it in a "chopper box" to gain entrance to the platform area. The chopper boxes were manned by vigilant uniformed guards to preclude the use of counterfeit tickets. In 1915 the ticket system was phased out and coin-of-the-realm accepted as direct payment.

The city celebrated its new transit line with enthusiasm "quite out of keeping with the Boston character, as it is generally interpreted," according to one decorous eyewitness description. And like its predecessor, the original subway of 1897, the Roxbury-Charlestown line was an immediate, large-scale success. True enough, persons living on the top floor of three-story apartments adjacent to the tracks had to be vigilant in lowering their window shades, and some realtors sourly reported that "For Rent" signs were appearing along the el's route more frequently than elsewhere. But the advent of the new transit line served to solidify property values in territories far beyond the immediate range of the line's alleged disadvantageous effects. Still, cries would frequently be heard that the elevated sections should be torn down and replaced with a subway.

Such carping aside, Boston had scooped America again in transit development—for the 1901 line was the nation's premier employment of multiple-unit electric-powered cars underground. New York, under whose sidewalks m.u. equipment would eventually proliferate, did not have a subway until 1904.

The Main Line El was to receive many additions and alterations to its original configuration, the first within a mere two months of its June 1901 opening. Turning off the Main Line just north of Dover Street station, this was an all-elevated right-of-way over Atlantic Avenue. It rejoined the original route near North Union Station and provided an alternate routing to the Tremont Street subway. It linked the two major railroad stations and provided access to the numerous steamship berths and ferryboat slips along the waterfront. Over the years, a variety of routings would appear on head-end destination boards—through trains in Sullivan-Dudley service *via* Atlantic Avenue, a special "Atlantic Circuit" train in loop service through the subway and over the waterfront el, a North Station-South Station shuttle. For a time in the beginning, trains from either Sullivan or Dudley ran over both el and subway and then looped back to the terminal of origin.

A construction view from 1907 when the Main Line El was being rerouted from the Tremont Street subway into its own Washington Street tunnel. Here the project is shown crossing the twin main lines of the New York Central and the New York, New Haven & Hartford Railroads, just west of South Station. (M.B.T.A.)

Rowe's Wharf station on the Atlantic Avenue El, Sept. 1921. (M.B.T.A.)

Nevertheless, in BE Ry's view of things, the Atlantic Avenue El was never an out-and-out success. It had bad luck, particularly in January, 1919, when a huge iron molasses tank belonging to the Purity Distilling Company on Commercial Street in the North End exploded. A two-*million* gallon wave of syrup surged into Atlantic Avenue, knocking out one support column of the el and weakening several others.* On September 30, 1938, the Atlantic Avenue El ran its last train. It is the only major transit line in Boston ever to be abandoned.

In 1909 the Main Line El was extended southward some 2½ miles from Dudley to a most impressive terminal station at Forest Hills, called the *"chef d'oeuvre"* of rapid transit development in Boston down to this time." The feature eliciting such favorable comment was poured concrete, as opposed to standard steel-girder construction. At Forest Hills, el-to-trolley transfers could be made to numerous points in the southwestern suburbs. At 5:16 A.M. on Monday, November 22nd, a gong sounded in the new station, whereat five freshly painted el cars departed for Sullivan Square, carrying 48 passengers and a bevy of BE Ry officials. "Running smooth as grease and every train on time," remarked trainmaster George Benjamin after the first day of operation.

The El company's planning probed northward beyond Sullivan Square to destinations in Malden and Melrose, and even Lynn. Yet the only northward extension ever to get beyond the discussion stage began service on March 15, 1919, when trains started running an additional elevated mile across Mystic River into a ter-

---

* Although a serious disaster involving loss of life, the "molasses explosion" has become a legend of sorts in Boston. Old-timers claim you can still *smell* its remains on hot summer days in the North End.

24

minal at Everett. Remarked at the time to be little more than a temporary arrangement—the terminal itself was far from elaborate, and downright shoddy compared to Forest Hills—it was to remain "temporary" for over 50 years.

Steel cars were introduced in 1907; by 1928 all the original wooden units were fittingly retired. The reason why steel cars were not ordered in 1901, when the line opened, is simple enough—the all-steel passenger car was not invented until 1903!

Over the years the el's car fleet was upgraded to incorporate state-of-the-art advances in transit technology and design. For instance, original equipment featured open-end platforms and manual-gate entry—generally called the "Manhattan type" arrangement, named for the popular New York el design. Cars with enclosed vestibules and automatic doors came later; in time the once-open platforms of the 1901-vintage cars were enclosed and

Forest Hills station under construction in August, 1909. Note single-truck open trolley. (M.B.T.A.) Lower photo: Its run from Everett over, a train of 01100 series cars on present-day Main Line El (Orange Line) heads out of Forest Hills station onto the tail track to change ends for the return trip. (Tom Nelligan photo)

In the spacious train shed at Charlestown's Sullivan Square, the Main Line El transfers passengers to multitudinous surface bus lines. Many users feel that the appearance of this edifice has a decidedly "European" cast. (Nelligan)

fitted with sliding doors. El cars were also equipped with "trip" devices designed to bring a train to a sudden stop should a motorman happen to run past a red signal. During its early years BE Ry rolling stock was painted maroon with gold trim, but by the mid-1920's this aristocratic livery had been replaced by a typi-

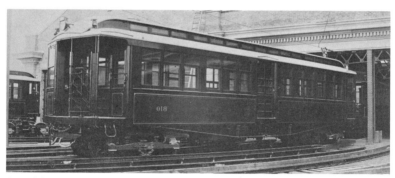

One of the original wooden cars of the Main Line El, No. 018 was built by Wason, and is shown here at Sullivan Square. When BE Ry eventually enclosed the open platforms, the fleet looked like No. 075, below. (Both photos, M.B.T.A.)

cal railroad-coach green, minus trim, striping, or any sort of ornamentation.

Yet by far the most important revision of the Main Line El took place just after seven years of operation, when trains were rerouted from the original Tremont Street subway into a brand-new $8 million, 1.23-mile tunnel under Washington Street. "The plan is unique in that it is designed for elevated cars only, no provision for the running of surface cars in the subway being made." The stations were well appointed and—to quote a noted contemporary architect—"of offensive decoration there was none." On Monday morning, November 30, 1908, trains departing from Sullivan and Dudley at 5:24 A.M. became the first revenue runs through the new tube. The final changeover from the Tremont Street route had been accomplished, again in a single week-end, by frantic activity reminiscent of 1901. The Tremont Street subway reverted at once to all-trolley status, its high platforms torn out and the link-up ramp at Pleasant Street disconnected.

One final note regarding the Main Line El: right at the start Boston appears to have had a positive fascination for coining and using very proper names for its various transit services. The Tremont Street Line, since it operated trolley cars underground, was dubbed "the subway;" while the Washington Street Line, which operated high-platform, third-rail pickup trains, was called "the tunnel." If anyone cared to challenge this distinction and usage he was referred to chapter 584 of the Acts of 1894 and chapter 534 of the Acts of 1902, where it was all spelled out with the utmost precision.

Against a backdrop of Charlestown architecture, a Forest Hills-bound train rounds the curve and drifts into City Square station. (Tom Nelligan)

27

Above: East Boston cars at Eliot Yard. No. 0501 and similar units replaced trolleys in tunnel service. (M.B.T.A.)

Right: Out of the blackness of the East Boston Tunnel, a four-car train of post-war 0500 St. Louis-built cars rumbles to a halt at the Aquarium station. (Tom Nelligan)

Vignette, opposite page: Tunnels built after completion of the original subway. Clockwise, from Park Street location, they are East Boston, Dorchester Extension, Washington Street, Beacon Hill. Dotted line is Atlantic Avenue, where the El once ran.

3. THE EAST BOSTON TUNNEL

FOR ITS TIME, the most ambitious transit project Boston ever undertook was a trolley tunnel under Boston Harbor. Because, while subaqueous tunnels are commonplace enough today, they surely were not in 1904.

The accepted method for tunneling through soft underwater silt is the Greathead Shield. This circular device, named for its British inventor, moves forward inside a pressurized air lock, and allows the tunnel shell to be constructed from within. Many of the river tunnels in New York, for instance, were built this way. But the

clay under Boston Harbor proved to be firmer than silt, so that a modified—but only slightly so—technique was used. The tunneling device itself, called a "roof shield," was a semi-circular steel vault also set-up within a pressurized atmosphere. The procedure was: two small pilot tunnels were dug in advance of the shield and shored up with heavy timbers. Inside these bores concrete footings for the final side walls were poured. Then, pushed by hydraulic jacks, the roof shield advanced, supported by rollers on the top of the pre-constructed footings. The vault of the shield itself shored up the cavity of the tunnel proper and, as soon as interior excavation was completed, the permanent structure was built, the roof shield doing double duty as a sort of mold. At an average weekly advance of 32 feet, it took two-and-a-half years to finish the mile-long project, 2,700 feet of which are actually under water. Four workmen lost their lives during the work; it cost three million in 1904 dollars; 61,000 cubic yards of concrete and 1,450 tons of steel were needed to complete the tunnel.

Howard Carsen, supervisor of the original subway, was named chief engineer on this project. When trolley cars began to run through the tube in December, 1904, it was the second* long distance underwater vehicular tunnel in America, and stood as a splendid accomplishment.

East Boston marked the tunnel opening with uncommon gusto. The night before official service began a formal dinner was held at Masonic Hall, and invited guests were treated to a tour through East Boston neighborhoods aboard ten brand-new BE Ry trolley cars—"similar to the ones now being used on the Brookline and Brighton boulevard lines"—by William A. Bancroft, president of BE Ry. Streets came alive with celebratory activity despite the fact that it was wintertime. Fireworks lighted the night sky. Then the fleet of cars dipped down into the new tunnel for a preview look at the object of the celebration. Of those present, nobody had a grander time through it all than Massachusetts Governor John L. Bates. Ten years earlier, as first-term representative from East Boston, he had skillfully maneuvered to have this district included in the 1894 legislation as both requiring and deserving of transit service. And despite strong disapproval of the route by BE Ry— President Bancroft claimed East Boston had been "saddled into the legislation"—here it was, ready for official inauguration.

---

* In 1890 the Grand Trunk R.R. built a tunnel under the St. Clair River between Port Huron, Michigan, and Sarnia, Ontario.

The morning after, December 30, 1904, motorman John Alexander left Lexington Street car barn in East Boston at 5:20 A.M. on trolley car No. 581. Picking up passengers en route, the car wound its way to Maverick Square, entered the new tunnel, and at 5:37 was discharging the historic first customers to pay their way under Boston Harbor—at Court Street in downtown Boston. The fare they paid, incidentally, was a penny higher than the El's regular five-cent tariff, this to help offset the costs of the tunnel. No. 588 from Chelsea on the Broadway Line came next, and the third trolley through the new tunnel was No. 407 from Orient Heights.

An immediate, noticeable effect of the opening of East Boston Tunnel was a serious drop-off of patronage on the municipally-operated ferry boats. A reporter commented that only teams of horses seemed to be using the old side-wheel steamers, now that the cars were running beneath the harbor bottom. Ironically, the eventual demise of the ferry boats was itself instrumental in the 1938 abandonment of BE Ry's own Atlantic Avenue Line.

The Court Street terminal layout was cumbersome. Trolleys had to "change ends" in the station before returning to Maverick and East Boston. This situation was rectified in 1916 by an extension crosstown, .41 miles, to Bowdoin Station. Here there was room for both a loop turnaround and an incline up and out to surface tracks in the middle of Cambridge Street, thus making possible through trolley service between, for example, Chelsea and Cambridge. The cost: $2.3 million.

Then, in the course of an April double-holiday weekend in 1924, the East Boston Line underwent the strangest metamorphosis of any Hub transit operation. Patrons of the line went home on Friday the 18th, the eve of Patriots' Day—a state holiday honoring the battles of Lexington and Concord—aboard their familiar trolley cars; but they returned to work on Monday morning, the day after Easter, riding brand-new steel m.u. trains which they could board and leave at platform level. Three years of planning and preliminary construction preceded this changeover.

As the final trolley rumbled clear of the tunnel at 8:30 P.M., Friday night, over 1,500 men were poised for work on a task so extensive that many observers doubted it could be done in time. Thousands of feet of Z-bar guard rail had to be removed and replaced by rails allowing the M.C.B.-type wheel flanges* of the new

---

* Wheel flanges machined to Master Car Builder specifications were of a different profile from the trolley wheels.

cars to negotiate the line. Old "special work"—340 feet of it—had to be ripped out, and 724 feet of new switches and crossovers installed. Nearly four miles of third rail had to be hoisted onto pre-set insulators, electrically connected, and tested. Fortunately, a new General Manager had come to the El in 1924, a man who would provide the transit system with more than thirty years of firm, knowledgeable leadership and who, many feel, directed the El to its peak of achievement. His name was Edward Dana (Harvard, '07). Dana not only saw the East Boston changeover through to on-time completion—he capped it off in verse appropriate to Patriots' Day:

> *Listen good friends and you shall read*
> *Of an all night toil on an urgent need.*
> *On the eighteenth of April in twenty-four*
> *Hardly a soul heard the hammer's roar—*
> *Or thought of the men who accomplished the deed.*

The first train of steel cars was operating at 1:00 A.M. Monday morning, April 21st. At 5:05 A.M. that same day Dana led a party of sleepy dignitaries aboard the first revenue train—out of Maverick, now totally rebuilt for transfer of passengers from the new high-platform trains to street cars at subway level.

The cars themselves, series 0500 built by Pullman, had already been tested on BE Ry's Cambridge subway (soon to be described), and thereafter through 1951 were maintained and serviced at the Eliot Shops of this route. Access between the two lines was *via* the former trolley-car incline at Bowdoin, a short haul (very slowly!) over street car trackage, and thence into the Cambridge subway at mid-point of Longfellow Bridge. This bizarre shunting operation was decorously conducted in the dark of night.

The 0500 cars were a poser for the Elevated's design staff, because the route had been built for trolleys: very sharp curves, very close clearances, and—in 1904—no premonition of the 1924 conversion. The grade in the tunnel was 5%, severe enough for trolleys but even more so for m.u. subway trains. The new cars seated 44 passengers, were short and narrow—47 x 8½ feet—and rode on small, 26-inch wheels, thereby saving a few inches of height. They were permanently coupled as two-car sets, each set sharing common electrical equipment to save weight. A single 0500-series subway car weighed but 44,000 pounds, whereas the final series of trolleys used in East Boston Tunnel weighed 45,000 pounds each.

Thus Boston's third rapid transit line opened for business in 1904, but twenty years later was transformed into something its original designers never imagined. Still its growth was not finished, and we will return to the East Boston Tunnel in the post-World War II era for more strange developments.

Electric motors are efficient and dependable, but they do require periodic maintenance. Here a BE Ry man rewinds the armature of a typical trolley car motor. (M.B.T.A.)

Bound for Lechmere Square, a two-car train of "picture window" P.C.C. cars heads up the Haymarket incline. (Tom Nelligan photo)

Vignette, opposite page: A "type 4" trolley is about to descend into the Tremont-Boylston subway at the incline located east of Arlington Street. Circa 1938. (M.B.T.A.)

Below: At North Station, Main Line El trains must negotiate a sharp ninety-degree turn before heading down the incline to the Washington Street tunnel. At street level in the scene can be glimpsed the skylight for a new underground station which the line will use when it is extended to Oak Grove in the near future, and the elevated structure shown here will be torn down. (Tom Nelligan photo)

4. SOME REFLECTIONS ON THE BOSTON EL

THE BOSTON ELEVATED RAILWAY was a stockholder corporation whose purpose, in free-enterprise parlance, was the earning of dividends for investors. Nevertheless, urban public transportation was, and continues to be, a social service not to be wholly understood within a profit-and-loss context. This angle of the matter explains, as much as anything else, the frictions that developed in Boston between citizen representatives and the overlords of the Elevated.

The public-private tug of war took place chiefly under the golden dome of the State House on Beacon Hill. In 1901, for instance, when BE Ry was in the first decade of its corporate existence, debate was underway on the proposed Washington Street tunnel for the Main Line El. "The state of Massachusetts is to become the servant of the corporation," thundered one legislator after pondering the provisions of an early proposal. Another—from a North Shore locale well beyond BE Ry's sphere of influence, decried the lack of opposition to certain features of a bill that were clearly beneficial to the corporation: "Only the other day a member from Boston told me he could not oppose this bill because he had 300 men working on the elevated. Where are the Boston members this morning? Many of them know they are owned by this great corporation."

During the same debate a Boston representative from Ward 11 stood up in the chamber and defended himself from what he considered to be libelous and defaming charges. He denied the accusation and denounced his accuser—and what was the infamy that generated such concern? "I claim he has assailed my reputation. He insinuates I was smoking cigars [belonging to] the Boston Elevated Railway."

The same BE Ry would, of course, eventually surrender its

35

status as a private corporation, an evolutionary process common to all U.S. cities in which private interests had launched subways and els early in the 20th century. In 1947 the properties, liabilities, assets and good name of the Boston El were transferred to a totally public agency—the Metropolitan Transit Authority. Yet between the halcyon days of profits both lucrative and automatic, and the advent of M.T.A., the Boston El wrote some interesting chapters in the history of American economics. Beginning in 1918, BE Ry—as did also some once-private transit companies in New York, Chicago and Philadelphia—moved into a hybrid status neither out-and-out *laissez faire* capitalism nor non-profit municipal service. Boston called it "public control."

Transit income from fares was fixed at five cents each by lease agreements which permitted BE Ry to operate its trains and trolleys into public-owned subway facilities. Money inflation during and after World War I eroded the company's financial position to the brink of receivership. To avoid this, the Massachusetts Public Service Commission, now the agency of jurisdiction, proposed that actual operating control of BE Ry be put in the hands of a "public" Board of Trustees. There was to be a municipal guarantee of a specified return on BE Ry securities. And more: the municipality would meet any deficit in transit operations, and a "floating fare" would be authorized which the trustees could peg at whatever figure was needed to meet expenses.

The proposal was highly controversial—indeed, of all the crises BE Ry and its successors struggled through, none evoked quite such sound and fury from Beacon Hill as this proposed public control act. "Rich investors are going to grow fat on the pennies of poor subway riders!" trumpeted one legislator. The very notion of upping the fare was, in 1918 Boston, as popular among the citizenry as, say, surgery. But whether or not public control was the proper response, surgery of some sort is what BE Ry needed. As the state P.S.C. put it: "Unusual conditions demand unusual remedies. The commission believes that in the present emergency private credit and private enterprise are unequal to the task and that no fundamental improvement can be accomplished unless the whole community puts its shoulder to the wheel and pulls the BE Ry out of the slough into which it is rapidly sinking. . . ."

The influential *Electric Railway Journal* agreed with this diagnosis: "The transportation system of the Boston Elevated Railway is not meeting the public needs, for the property has not been kept in good, modern operating condition, the net earnings are shrinking, the service is poor and the credit is gone."

Legislative outrage simmered down to resignation; the public control bill became law in May. BE Ry President Matthew C. Brush called it the "biggest, strongest, finest piece of legislation ever passed in the electric railway field." Brokers quickly pointed out to their clients that the new law placed BE Ry "paper" on a plane only slightly less stable than United States treasury bonds. On August 1st the fare was raised to seven cents and, in 1919, to ten cents.

Economic difficulties aside, BE Ry did accomplish some memorable things during its fifty-odd years of existence, earning high marks for equipment design, notably for a vehicle that excited the entire traction world. This was the "center-entrance car" designed especially for service in the trolley subways. The first of these appeared on the property in 1915 as motorless trailers requiring a conventional trolley for power. Then, beginning in 1917, the initial units of a fleet of 405 center-entrance *motor* cars were delivered by Brill and Laconia. They were big—almost 49 feet long—had an acceleration and braking rate of 1.75 mphps. Four General Electric No. 247 motors powered arch bar trucks on 24-inch wheels. Trolley poles mounted in an unusual "reversed" manner made for easy changing in the restricted confines of the subway. A motorman and a conductor were the normal complement in passenger service. Of all the vehicles designed for service in Boston over the years, the bulky and awkward-looking center-entrance cars remain the favorites of many who knew them. "They got up heat

A three-car train of center-entrance cars heads for the subway along Commonwealth Avenue. This is the service for which the cars will be best remembered, heavy-duty operation into the Tremont-Boylston subway. (M.B.T.A.)

real good on cold mornings," a retired motorman recently remarked, adding, "I'd say they were our best cars for getting through heavy snow."

The center-entrance motors were initially assigned to East Boston Tunnel service, but they are best remembered running outdoors in three-car multiple-unit trains on the Beacon Street and Commonwealth Avenue routes, from which they dove into the original subway complex. The wide center doors were ideal for the fast loading and unloading demanded of them at the Park and Boylston stations. Also, just prior to their acquisition, the original subway had been enlarged almost to its present day proportions.

In 1912 a 1.8-mile elevated route was opened, from the Haymarket incline to Lechmere Square in Cambridge. Then in 1914 a very important westward leg was spliced onto the original Tremont Street Line. Beyond the Public Gardens incline—a new and different Public Gardens incline, the original one being incompatible with the expansion plans—a two-track tunnel was run under Boylston Street through Back Bay to a point just east of Governor (now Kenmore) Square. Service to this quarter of the city had long been discussed; a proposal called the Riverbank Subway at one time seemed to be on the verge of construction. This would have been a totally new trolley subway from Park Street, beneath Beacon Hill to the bank of the Charles River, and thence west. It was never built. (Instead, the Boylston Street subway today provides service to Brookline, Allston and Brighton.) In 1932 another addition extended the subway through and beyond Kenmore Square to two different inclines—one at Blandford Street and Commonwealth Avenue, and the other at Beacon and St. Mary's Streets. This is the present limit of the subway.

An oddity of sorts is that the station at Kenmore Square was built with the thought of someday converting the entire trolley subway to high platform standards, as had been done on the East Boston Line. Consequently, the center pair of tracks in the four-track facility (see diagram) was constructed on raised supports. (If these are ever removed, the alignment will be perfect for high platform cars.) The outside pair of tracks would always be for street cars, it was reasoned, thus a return loop was built so that trolleys on these tracks could transfer passengers at Kenmore to the subway, and afterward return from whence they came.

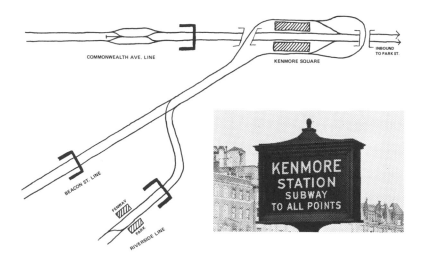

COMMONWEALTH AVE. LINE

KENMORE SQUARE

INBOUND TO PARK ST.

BEACON ST. LINE

FENWAY

PARK

RIVERSIDE LINE

KENMORE STATION SUBWAY TO ALL POINTS

These westward extensions of the trolley subway have since become a heavily trafficked line, but one of its more unusual "operations" took place the night of December 13, 1917, when intervals between trains were less cramped. One Daniel Kinnally of Chelsea was making last-minute deliveries in the Fenway area. He left his horse and wagon untended and untethered while he quickly ran into an apartment building. The horse—whose name, at this remove, is unknown—took off on his or her own equine responsibility. Horse and wagon, the latter racketing across the crossties, headed into the incline at Kenmore Square. The agent at the first station, Massachusetts Avenue, was notified of the unscheduled movement. Timidly, he stepped onto the track to intercept the runaway. Out of the gloom galloped the strange consist, looking for all the world like a fugitive from *Ben Hur*. Intrepid agent David Berry thus became the first transit employee on record ever to flag a horse in the Boylston Street subway.

Speaking of BE Ry employees, it should be noted that they were a well-trained corps, generally eliciting favorable public comment for courtesy and helpfulness. Not to perfection, perhaps, but the fact is that the Elevated took pains to prescribe a pleasant mode of behavior for its personnel. A 1917 instruction booklet contains, for example, this reminder: "The use of the word PLEASE in directing the actions of passengers makes the difference between an order and a request—makes the difference between courtesy and curtness."

As far back as 1901, General Bancroft had addressed himself to the question of the standards to be upheld by BE Ry employees. His qualifications included: "Our conductors must be presentable, for the very appearance of some men gives offense quickly in a cultured community. These men must have all their fingers and thumbs, and now-a-days they must have all their toes also." There was a further norm to be met: the possession of "a reasonable number of either real or artificial teeth."

Center-entrance car No. 6257 poses at Lake Street Shelter together with BE Ry employees selected, presumably, in keeping with General Bancroft's qualifications. The March, 1921, scene shows the Commonwealth Avenue transfer point to cars of the Middlesex & Boston Street Ry before the present off-street terminal was constructed. (M.B.T.A.) Vignette, opposite page: On Longfellow Bridge en route to Cambridge, a train of 01400 cars at speed. (Nelligan)

5. ACROSS THE RIVER TO CAMBRIDGE

TALK OF, and plans for, a rapid transit line in Cambridge also date back to the earliest era of subways in Boston. The enabling legislation of 1894, resulting in the original 1897 subway, stipulated also that the Boston Transit Commission provide for a new bridge over the Charles River, this to accommodate both street traffic *and* a transit line. Such a bridge was begun in July, 1900, and formally dedicated in 1907, but the built-in transit right-of-way in the center of the $2.6-million span remained unused for five years thereafter.

Preparatory talk was of an elevated line, although it soon became clear that in Cambridge a subway would be better. Work on the line did not, however, begin until 1909 because a smouldering feud had first to be resolved concerning the number of stations to be built on sections of the line in Cambridge proper. Local residents, championed by Cambridge's Mayor Wardwell, wanted the subway to serve *their* needs with five stations, at least, between Harvard Square and the Charles River. Opposed were suburbanites living beyond Harvard Square. They wanted a through-express route into Boston for *their* convenience—surely a single station in Cambridge would suffice, obviously at Central Square, where there were excellent transfer facilities to street cars bound for Brookline and Newton. "I will not stand idly by and see our community become a mere thoroughfare for those who live in the country," declared an irate Cambridge resident, whose opinion reflected the majority of his neighbors.

The conflict raged. Outside consultants became embroiled even unto judicial review, and the issue was settled by a compromise—on *two* stations. The Cambridge faction clinched matters by marshaling an impressive array of academic talent asserting that a long, station-free subway would become so charged with "mephitic exhalations" as to present a perilous health hazard for riders.

The line was plotted to run from Harvard Square to a point *beneath* the Park Street station of the Tremont Street subway, this after an earlier proposal to make Scollay Square the Boston terminal. The project involved four construction phases. First and second, or vice versa, a deep underground tunnel would be built through Beacon Hill by the Transit Commission plus, as noted above, the Charles River Bridge. For the rest, a short, elevated link-up between the Beacon Hill tunnel and the bridge would be erected by Boston Elevated Railway, likewise responsible for the subway portion in Cambridge. The route *in toto* was assigned two technical labels: named in Boston proper the "Cambridge Connector," across the river it became the "Cambridge Main Street Subway." The press lamented anew how Boston risked "national ridicule" for its hair-splitting over subway nomenclature.

"Beacon Hill is presumably a glacial formation," ventured a 1911 issue of *Scientific American,* editorially, in comment on the geology, not the politics, of the deep tunnel route. This section of the project required precision engineering. A roof shield weighing 65 tons was used to force a 32-foot diameter bore directly under the city's top-drawer residential area. At its deepest point, the floor of the tunnel rests a hundred feet below street level; the tunneling cut across numerous artesian wells dating from pre-Revolutionary days. By contract provision, the bore could have been built inside an airlock with artificially pressurized atmosphere, but the ground proved to be sufficiently firm—as the engineers hopefully expected —so that the complex and costly "extra" of an airlock was unnecessary. Even though a portion of the tunnel had to be negotiated through a 4000-foot radius arc, it "came out" within six inches of its calculated position. Come Saturday morning, March 23, 1912, the Cambridge line—by both its names—was ready. The bill for 3.20 miles of construction came to $11,750,000.

Mrs. Mary Collett, of Revere Street, Cambridge, after standing in line at Harvard Square since 3:00 A.M., purchased the first ticket. Somehow, the first man to pay a fare was William Dwyer, a Cambridge physician routinely on his way home after making an emergency night call, who became curious about the people and the noise in Harvard Square. At 5:10 A.M. a three-car train moved into the departure track on the lower of the two levels in Harvard Square station, but when officials calculated the size of the crowd,

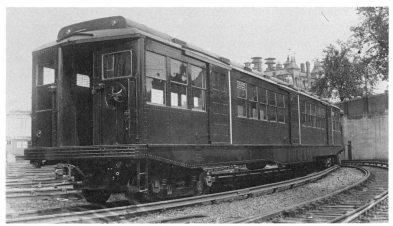

Fresh from its builder in 1928, a 69-foot car for the Cambridge-Dorchester Line poses for the photographer in Eliot Yard. (M.B.T.A.)

a fourth car was quickly added. At 5:20 passengers were let into the station, and on the dot of 5:24 the four cars, numbered 0618, 0614, 0620 and 0623, accelerated into the eight-minute run to a familiar destination with a brand-new name—"Park Street Under." Motorman William Miles was at the controller; 286 passengers made the trip. Accounts of this inaugural run spoke of the "varsity-like behavior" of the riders and suggested that "perhaps the crimson trimmings of the Harvard station had a tendency to inspire the passengers upon the first train to give vent to this overflow of enthusiasm."

The El Company and its successors have since dispatched thousands upon thousands of trains over the Cambridge Line. None can conceivably compare with the extraordinary run of "train number 86" narrated by science-fiction writer A. J. Deutsch in a story entitled *A Subway Named Mobius.** En route to Cambridge No. 86 disappears for several weeks, all the while activating signals and existing in a heard-but-not-seen state throughout the entire Boston subway complex. Mathematicians versed in topology may argue that such a run is entirely possible. Meanwhile, let *us* return to 1912.

The cars designed for the Cambridge subway were a departure from the then existing equipment anywhere in the U.S. Externally,

---

* Published December, 1950, in *Astounding Science Fiction.* Reprinted, 1971, in *Where Do We Go from Here?* edited by Isaac Asimov. New York: Doubleday & Company, Inc.

the noticeable difference was that they had no vestibules at the ends, but doors spaced evenly along the sides. Also, they were both longer and wider than cars on BE Ry's older Main Line El. Their basic design was later adopted by the Brooklyn Rapid Transit Company for cars to operate on its new lines in the years succeeding 1913.

The first 40 "Cambridge" cars were built by the Standard Steel Car Company. Each measured 69 feet, 2½ inches long and 9 feet, 6 inches wide at the door sills, in contrast to the typical Main Line car of 46-foot length, 8-foot-7½-inch width. An empty Cambridge car weighed 85,900 pounds and had seats for 72 passengers . . . *vs.* 70,000 pounds, 44 passengers. The newcomers ran on Brill No. 27 M.C.B. trucks, one of which was a motor truck with 34-inch wheels, the other a trailer with 31-inch wheels. Power for the motor trucks came from two Westinghouse 200 hp, No. 300B motors geared 20:63 for a free-running speed of 45 mph.

For the advantages gained by the adoption of a different set of specifications for the new line there was a corresponding disadvantage. True enough, the near-ten-foot width of the Cambridge cars allowed for more passengers per car, and the line's wide-radius curves meant that better speeds could be maintained. But, henceforth, equipment could never be routinely interchanged between

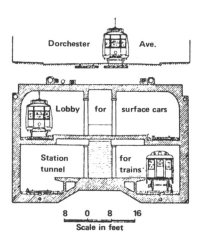

Above: Cross-section of Broadway station, Dorchester Extension. At right: A Harvard-Ashmont train just out of Beacon Hill tunnel and into Charles Street station over a short section of elevated track. (Nelligan)

Beyond Tower Q at Ashmont terminal is a double crossover and three tail tracks where Cambridge-Dorchester trains can change ends. Beyond the tail tracks is Codman Yard, where equipment is stored. Off to the left can be seen an ex-Dallas double-ender bound for Mattapan Square on the "high speed" line. (Tom Nelligan photo)

the two high-platform lines. When Main Line El cars were at one time assigned to the Cambridge run, during an equipment shortage, they had first to be equipped with temporary steel extension plates at the door sills to bridge the gaps resulting when cars 9-feet wide stopped at platforms built to handle the new, wider units. (Obviously 10-foot-wide cars could never run on a line built to operate 9-footers!) In short, the need to maintain separate car fleets over the years would be a chronic bother, and we noted above that when the East Boston Line was converted to high-platform standards in 1924, its particular dimensions added yet another set of specifications to BE Ry's fleet.

The Cambridge-Park Street Under subway was extended bit-by-bit beyond Park Street toward South Boston. By December of 1917 a tunnel under the Fort Point Channel—a surprisingly complex and difficult job—brought the line to Broadway Station *in* South Boston. Here a massive underground transfer facility was built so that street cars from all points zoomed down an incline directly into the mezzanine level of the station.

45

Harvard vs. Yale, 1921. Throng of spectators debarks from Cambridge-Dorchester train in Eliot Yard only a few steps from the stadium. (M.B.T.A.)

Year 1923—still another bill cleared the legislature, enabling still another extension of the Cambridge Connector, this time over the right-of-way of the Shawmut Branch to Dorchester of the New York, New Haven and Hartford Railroad. There were complaints as usual, chiefly from Milton residents irked at losing direct steam-train service into South Station; also many Dorchester residents would have preferred a subway under Dorchester Avenue itself rather than the less accessible Shawmut Branch. But the line was welcome nonetheless, and nobody was more pleased when a ceremonial train arrived at Fields Corner on November 4, 1927, than one Charles Ufford. . . .

For 30 years he had championed the cause of rapid transit to his native Dorchester. He spoke before civic groups, showed lantern slides to luncheons, wrote letters to legislators, and in general kept up pressure for the cause he believed in. Ufford was neither special-pleader nor professional lobbyist, just an ordinary citizen who had a transit dream, and rode it through to actuality. "I stand today a happy man," said he at the official ceremony. Alas, a flawed happiness—because BE Ry, rerouting its many surface car lines in the Dorchester area, scheduled the Norfolk Street Line (which served Ufford's neighborhood) into the Dudley station of the Main Line El rather than a station on the new Dorchester Extension!

The following year service was extended to Ashmont and beyond when a "high-speed" trolley line was built to connect with the Cambridge-Dorchester Line, serving sections of Milton and terminating at Mattapan Square. In all, the Dorchester extension, including the Mattapan shuttle, marked the first time an electric rapid transit line was substituted for an older steam-railroad commuter line, a practice that today has become standard in the planning of new transit facilities.

Between 1911 and 1928 BE Ry took delivery of 155 subway cars to serve this line. Its operations remained virtually unchanged until the Quincy Line opened in 1971. One special service, strictly seasonal, involved the routing of trains beyond Harvard Square terminal through Eliot Yard, thence up to a station platform located adjacent to Boylston Street—from which football fans could meander into Harvard Stadium across a short bridge.

The Cambridge Subway offered Bostonians yet another opportunity to exercise their penchant for precise and proper terminology. The transfer point at Park Street was located beneath the time-honored terminal of the Tremont Street subway, but it just wouldn't do to call the new tunnel station simply "Park Street." Instead the more exact title was selected, and a common usage coined that would serve uncertain natives in need of orientation en route, but which tended to create bewilderment and confusion when proffered to out-of-towners unfamiliar with the Boston idiom: "Change at Park Street Under!"

During rush hour the Mattapan-Ashmont "high speed" line operates trolleys on very close headways. But in the quiet of midday it resembles nothing so much as a sleepy interurban line from years gone by. Imagine, in the scene above, a Niles-built combine with deck roof in place of the P.C.C. leaving Capen Street station.
(Tom Nelligan photo)

Trolley is last in line of traffic backed up at intersection of Massachusetts and Huntington avenues during construction of subway under Huntington. It's 1939, and one of the movies at the Uptown Theatre (left background) features a once favorite Boston repertory actor, Archie Leach, already one of America's favorites as Cary Grant. (M.B.T.A.)

Vignette, opposite page: During World War II, Boston El recruited women to fill in for regular employees who were in the services. (M.B.T.A.)

Below: Inbound from Riverside, three of the "picture window" P.C.C.s pause at Park Street. The custom designed left-hand door can be seen in this view. (Tom Nelligan)

6. THE 'FORTIES AND 'FIFTIES

THREE TRANSIT EXTENSIONS of these years deserve mention— one in particular providing an in-depth look at Boston's distinctive political style. Talk about a Huntington Avenue Subway bubbled and simmered for decades. When, in 1933, Mayor James Michael Curley proposed an $8.5 million subway linking Copley Square and the Museum of Fine Arts, he sparked an on-again-off-again debate enduring into 1941, when a line so named actually opened for business. In the trough of the '29 depression, BE Ry Chairman Bernard J. Rothwell was aghast at the thought. He claimed it would add $375,000 to the El's annual operating deficit. Even the precise length of the line was strenuously debated, productive of various suggestions, each with its own price tag. The line should go all the way to the museum . . . no, it should end at West Newton Street . . . or, how about Massachusetts Avenue?

As built, the line peeled off the Boylston Street subway west of Copley station, and by way of a highly unsatisfactory "flat junction" which forced westbound Huntington Avenue cars to cross the eastbound main at grade. It then twisted under the Boston & Albany railroad yard and below Huntington Avenue to an incline at Opera Place. An advantage, however, was that the new line permitted abandonment of the old incline at Public Gardens, thus eliminating surface cars from considerable downtown-Back Bay area.

Evening of February 15, 1941. A "type 4" trolley, No. 5364, rumbles across temporary girders over the still-abuilding incline. Once the car cleared, men began removing the temporary steel work, opening an access to the subway tunnel. At 2:30 the following afternoon a "last spike" ceremony tied the new subway to the old street-car line. Suitable "brass hats" boarded a 3-car train of center-entrance cars officially to open the new facility. At 3:25

P.M. the first revenue train departed Opera Place, one of the *very* few times that a Boston transit extension did *not* begin regular service at the crack of dawn. Notably, the Huntington Avenue Line was the second largest WPA project ever completed, topped only by New York's LaGuardia Airport. Of its $7 million cost, $5 million came from Washington, and $5 million of the total spent was wages "for the labor of 2,000 men who might otherwise have been on the city's welfare rolls for the past three years."

Boston's memorable center-entrance cars had their last hurrah on the Huntington Avenue inaugural. Through the early 1930s a committee within the street railway industry had been working on designs for cars supposedly to be the industry's *riposte* to the encroaching motorbus. The effort turned out to be one of the only times in the urban transit history when a common design *did* evolve. It could be used or adapted for service in varied cities and systems. Not that the gasoline-fuelled bus would vanish because of a new street car design! Nevertheless, this example of wisdom after the fact does not detract from the excellence of the car which the President's Conference Committee of the American Transit Association developed. A single-ended streamlined body, a multi-notch foot-operated controller, resilient wheels and other improvements distinguished what came to be known as the "P.C.C. car."

The first revenue units were built for New York's Brooklyn and Queens Transit Corporation in 1936 by the St. Louis Car Company. The following year St. Louis delivered a single P.C.C. to the Boston El. Numbered 3001—and popularly called the "Queen Mary"—it convinced El management that this was their car of the future. In 1941 BE Ry took delivery of a 20-car fleet of P.C.C.s manufactured by Pullman-Standard. Although not equipped for m.u. operation, they proved what had been suspected from experience with No. 3001—that the P.C.C. was a most appropriate replacement vehicle for the center-entrance car. During World War II, the War Production Board authorized BE Ry to reorder P.C.C.s in substantial numbers. These later ones *were* wired for m.u. train operation; they put the quietus to the veteran center-entrance cars in heavy-duty subway service. The last of the center-entrance type to carry passengers anyplace in Boston pulled down its pole in 1953, years after the breed had been retired from subway service.

A still later order for 50 "picture window" P.C.C.s was delivered in 1951. In 1958-59 Boston bought 25 second-hand double-ended P.C.C.s from the Dallas Railway & Terminal Company, so that through the '50s trolley cars were eliminated from all routes that did not feed the Tremont-Boylston subway—and even a few that did! The policy was to restrict the subway itself to the heavy patronage lines, and let other routes be bus-feeder operations. As none of the lines entering the tube *via* the Broadway (*nee* Pleasant Street) incline carried heavy traffic, it was abandoned in 1962. (A slight qualification: one trolley line still very much in business but *not* tied into the Central Subway is the Mattapan-Ashmont shuttle.)

In Boston the P.C.C. cars have performed well, if not ideally. The standard single-ended cars had to be equipped with left-side doors for the loading and discharge of passengers at several stations with left-hand platforms. Actually, the chief criticism leveled at the P.C.C. in Boston service has to be that it does not perform flawlessly during rush-hour loading at busy stations, specifically because the door arrangement was never designed for such service. Eventually, the two classes of P.C.C.s originally ordered without m.u. controls were so equipped, so that now the only cars that do not "train" are the ex-Dallas double-enders.

During 1945 the legislature voted approval and 1952 saw service extended beyond Maverick Station over the right-of-way of an abandoned narrow-gauge railroad—the 3-foot gauge Boston, Revere Beach & Lynn, defunct as of 1940.* The transit line built on a portion of its right-of-way—as far as Orient Heights in '52, Revere Beach in '54—is unique on two counts. For one, the first station beyond Maverick serves Logan Airport. Though a short bus ride separates the station from the airplanes, it is nevertheless the first urban transit line in the U.S. even to have come close to serving a commercial airfield. Another distinction of the line is its system of current collection, which changes beyond Maverick from third rail to, of all things, overhead catenary. The argument cited to explain this anomaly is the danger of icing on a third-rail installation so close to the ocean. The line does indeed run close to the shore, so that its passengers have the most scenic ride of all Boston transit patrons!

St. Louis-built cars—40 of them—were ordered to equip this extension, and all the 924-vintage cars were dolled up with panto-

---

* Had the BRB&L survived a few more months, the press of wartime traffic would surely have given the line a reprieve, and the face of transit in Boston thus might be very different today.

A two-car set of 1924 East Boston cars. The picture shows pantograph and massively proportioned headlights installed on the permanently coupled units after service was extended to Revere Beach. (M.B.T.A.) Bottom photo: In the long shadows of a late winter afternoon, a four-car train of St. Louis-built cars waits the call to service on the East Boston Line. (Tom Nelligan photo) Both scenes are in Orient Heights Yard.

graphs and headlights. Together the two fleets serve the line. As part of the extension a repair shop was built at Orient Heights, whereat the practice of maintaining East Boston cars at Eliot Shops was discontinued. The Cambridge Street incline at Bowdoin Square was at this time sealed off.

On July 1, 1959, yet another extension of the time-honored Tremont-Boylston subway was formally dedicated. The New York Central Railroad thankfully sold to M.T.A. a 9.4-mile grade-free right-of-way through Brookline and Newton for this, the first transit tentacle reaching out to Route 128, a six-lane peripheral highway experiencing a development boom as the "main street" of the U.S. electronics industry. The Riverside Line, as it has since been called, marked the first time P.C.C. cars operated over a lengthy, limited-stop route in Boston—not without criticism, because the street cars do not provide as fast or comfortable a ride under such conditions as conventional high-platform equipment. But Riverside was built cheaply, at a time when few cities were investing in any transport facilities other than highways. The line has functioned virtually without new equipment even though it is the longest transit route ever put into service all at one time in Boston. To free up the necessary P.C.C. cars, buses were assigned to street car routes in Cambridge and, it might be said, the ex-Dallas units were bought to liberate still more cars for Riverside.

Withal, the Riverside Line was a success from the start, but not as M.T.A. expected! The forecasts had it that the bulk of patronage would come from Brookline stations, but the more distant Newton stops drew so much the larger crowds that the Riverside storage yard quickly had to be enlarged to four times its original size. Indeed, the rumble of prior objections by Newton city officials was soon drowned out by the rumble of trains as the facility became accepted as a valuable asset to the community.

On the Glorious Fourth, 1959—three days after the line's official dedication—P.C.C. car No. 3295 led a three-car train out of Riverside Terminal at 6:50 A.M. When it reached Park Street at 7:25 the line was publicly in operation. Most of the historic first paying customers were "traction" buffs delighted beyond words to participate in the opening of a *new* trolley line in a decade when the more usual events were abandonments, cutbacks and bus substitutions.

The decade of the '50s also saw the purchase of 100 new Pullman-Standard cars for the Main Line El. Numbered in the 01100 series, they dispatched all but a handful of the older cars to the scrap heap. These few were retained to help out during rush hours on into the early 1960s, but today all service on the line is provided by the 01100 P-S cars.

But these achievements of a decade are prosy, however satisfactory. During the '50s the M.T.A. inspired the first song of the Boston subway since General Manager Dana's quoted on page 32. Composed and written by Jacqueline Steiner and Bess Hawes, it describes what happened to Charlie. Caught broke on a train as M.T.A.'s fare increase of five cents takes effect, Charlie seems fated to ride forever 'neath the streets of Boston, subsisting on the sandwich his wife thrusts daily through the car window as his train goes rumblin' through Scollay Square. As recorded for Capitol Records by the Kingston Trio, *THE M.T.A.* plummeted to popularity nation-wide. For the weeks that the record "made the charts," America became aware of the Boston subway as never before and, perhaps, of the need everywhere for effective urban mass transit. Could Oliver Wendell Holmes have done more?

Reaching out to Riverside, a three-car train on ex-NYC right-of-way in the Newtons.

Near Coolidge Corner, car No. 3288 poses against a background of the Beacon Street center-of-the-road trackage just traversed. (All photos, Tom Nelligan)

Car No. 3084 on the incline to Beacon Street shows off clean lines of war-time P.C.C. model, favorite of many traction buffs, unmarred by standee windows.

Rush hour is about over, and the storage yard at Riverside is filling up with cars, their assignments over for the day. M.B.T.A. plans to replace P.C.C.s on this line with new articulated cars based on designs developed in Germany over the past two decades.

7. BEYOND THE 'SEVENTIES

Iɴ 1963 the M.T.A. took delivery of 92 new lightweight cars—also built by Pullman-Standard—to completely re-equip the Cambridge-Dorchester Line. The following year, an idea that had germinated during a series of "Citizen Seminars" at Boston College took root, whereby the M.T.A. service district of 14 cities and towns was enlarged to 79. The older authority, M.T.A. itself, was succeeded by the present Massachusetts Bay Transportation Authority—M.B.T.A., or just plain "T", as its image-makers would have us say. Soon afterward the new authority adopted a color code to identify the various transit services: red is now the designation for the Cambridge-Dorchester Line, orange for the Main Line El, blue for East Boston and green for the trolley subway.

As part of a more colorful approach, the "T" began to repaint its rolling stock—including the orange P.C.C. cars—in neutral shades of grey, a less than aesthetic triumph. Eventually, and sensibly, the "T" refurbished its vehicles in color corresponding to the code of the line on which they operate. A total success on all counts, though, is a program of station modernization begun in 1967. *Time* magazine, whose staffers ride to work on the subways of New York City, felt that the Arlington Street face-lift—the first in the program—provided ample evidence that underground railways need not be as gloomy and depressing as they presently are in Gotham.*

As this is being written, M.B.T.A. crews are at work on a project called "Haymarket North"—a massive extension of the Main Line El, or Orange Line, to the Malden-Melrose border sharing the right-of-way of the Boston and Maine Railroad's Reading Branch. This project, financed through the 1964 bonding

---

* Blue Line's Airport station photomural, in vignette above, shows style of graphics used in station modernization.

The final two-car set of the 1963 01400 series cars came equipped with an experimental one-piece cast fiberglass end. The scene is Eliot Yard, Cambridge, destined to be the site of John F. Kennedy Memorial Library after completion of a new South Bay Maintenance Center in South Boston. (Author photos)

authorization, will enable the authority to tear down the entire elevated line from Haymarket to Everett—that very same structure "which the Boston elevated company has been allowed to disfigure and darken our streets with . . ." In its place will be an underwater passage of the Charles River *via* a modern, newly built transit line. At the southern end of the Washington Street tunnel, work is virtually complete on the "South Cove by-pass"—a tunnel connector which will some day enable Orange Line trains to eschew the elevated route through Dudley and reach Forest Hills, and beyond, over a new right-of-way.

Funds are available to continue the South Shore Line to Braintree; and the 1971 authorization envisions Orange Line service to West Roxbury and Needham, replacement of the 1924 cars on the Blue Line (locally nicknamed the "Dr. Zhivago cars") and extension also of the line beyond Revere to Pines River. Perhaps of greatest interest is that the $124 million in new bonding authorization voted by the legislature in 1971 specifies $30 million for refurbishing the Boylston-Tremont subway, including a replacement vehicle for the P.C.C. car. Most likely to be selected is a double-ended, articulated car patterned largely on European—and especially German—developments over the past few years.

And so the future looks like a busy time for the successors to Henry Whitney, William Bancroft, S. S. Neff and Edward Dana. So much remains to be done, thought through and achieved in Boston and elsewhere, if urban America in the 1970's is to have the full benefits which modern rapid transit can provide, that the really critical problems have not even been touched on above.

But our topic has not been the widespread urgencies

56

of the future, but the accomplishments of the past in Boston, a heritage compounded of men and machines and deeds. And how to sum up what it means in our lives? Is it the screech of wheel flanges as a train of P.C.C. cars heels into the loop at Park Street? Is it the sight of lighted windows on a Cambridge-Dorchester train gliding over Longfellow Bridge in the settling dusk of a late November afternoon? Is it the experience of hundreds of passengers streaming out of a Main Line El train at Sullivan Square, and catching buses for Medford, Melrose, and Everett? It is these things, and more—the sight of a lone center-entrance car parked silently outside Arborway car barn awaiting infrequent calls to work car assignments; the homey feel and warmth of a train of 0500s at Airport station after you've been out of town for a spell. It's all the sights and sounds and remembrances of things familiar and things gone by which contribute in part to the rich experience of life itself.

The old information booth at Park Street, haven for out-of-towners lost in the complexities of Boston subway. Light from windows and destination board of center-entrance trolley can be glimpsed in background. (M.B.T.A.)

*Above: Action on the South Shore Line!
Train at left heads into North Quincy
station as outbound Quincy Center train
rips by on roadbed of welded rail and
concrete ties. (Tom Nelligan photo)*

*At right: A fleet of 1903-era trolleys still
serves M.B.T.A. as snow plows. No. 5159,
with six inches or more of fresh snow
forecast by morning, prepares to earn her
keep. (Author photo)*

SUBWAY EQUIPMENT ROSTER

I. The Main Line Elevated (Orange Line)

Numbers	Builder	Year	Motors	Weight	Status	Notes
01-033	Wason	1899	2/Wh. #50	59,290	retired	
034-078	St. Louis	1899	2/Wh. #50	59,290	retired	
079-0100	Bradley	1899	2/Wh. #50	59,290	retired	
0101-0150	Wason	1903	2/Wh. #50	59,290	retired	1
0151-0174	St. Louis	1904	2/GE #68F	68,125	retired	2
0175-0219	Pressed Steel	1906	2/Wh. #301D	67,602	retired	5
0220-0239	Pressed Steel	1911	2/Wh. #301D	69,685	retired	3
0240-0264	A.C.F.	1914	2/Wh. #301D	71,557	retired	
0265-0294	Pressed Steel	1914	2/Wh. #301D	71,457	retired	
0295-0336	Pressed Steel	1917	2/GE #259	66,383	retired	4
0337-0401	Pressed Steel	1921	2/GE #259	70,108	retired	
0901-0974	Laconia	1927	2/Wh. #301D	69,460	retired	
0976-01000	Wason	1928	2/Wh. #301D	70,020	retired	5
01100-01199	Pullman	1957	4/GE #1250A1	57,540	in service	6, 7

II. The Cambridge-Dorchester-South Shore Line (Red Line)

Numbers	Builder	Year	Motors	Weight	Status	Notes
0600-0639	Standard Steel	1911	2/Wh. #300D	86,432	retired	
0640-0659	Laconia	1912	2/Wh. #212H	86,407	retired	8
0660-0694	Pressed Steel	1919	2/Wh. #577P	86,412	retired	
0695-0754	Bradley	1928	2/Wh. #577P	85,051	retired	9, 10
01400-01445	Pullman	1963	4/GE #1250F	70,000+	in service	7, 12
01446-01491	Pullman	1963	4/Wh. #1454G	70,000+	in service	7, 11, 12
01500-01523	Pullman	1969	4/Wh. 'Tracpak'	67,602	in service	12, 13
01600-01651	Pullman	1969	4/Wh. 'Tracpak'	—	in service	7, 12, 13, 23

III. The Boylston-Tremont Trolley Subway (Green Line)

In the early years of the trolley subway, many different classes and kinds of street cars operated into the facility. Only the center-entrance and P.C.C. cars are shown in this roster, however, since they are principally identified as especially designed or built for subway service.

6000-6049	Brill	1917	4/GE #247H	45,000	retired	27
6050-6099	Laconia	1917	4/GE #247H	45,000	retired	
6100-6299	Kuhlman	1918	4/GE #247H	45,000	retired	14
6300-6404	Laconia/Kuhlman	1920	4/GE #247H	45,000	retired	25
7000-7224	Brill/Laconia/ Kuhlman	1915-1918	none	26,000	retired	
3001	St. Louis	1936	4/GE #1198	34,020	retired	15, 21,28
3002-3021	Pullman	1941	4/Wh. #1432	36,580	in service	16
3022-3071	Pullman	1944	4/Wh. #1432	38,860	in service	
3072-3096	Pullman	1944	4/Wh. #1432	39,700	in service	
3097-3146	Pullman	1945	4/GE #1198	39,020/ 40,055	in service	
3147-3171	Pullman	1945	4/GE #1198	39,800	in service	
3172-3196	Pullman	1945	4/GE #1220	40,195	in service	
3197-3221	Pullman	1945	4/GE #1220	40,874	in service	18, 19
3222-3271	Pullman	1945	4/Wh. #1432	39,855/ 40,035	in service	17
3272-3321	Pullman	1951	4/GE #1224	40,280	in service	19, 26
3322-3346	Pullman	1945	4/Wh. AG114-32	39,360	in service	20, 21

IV. The East Boston-Revere Beach Line (Blue Line)

Only cars operated on the line after the 1924 upgrading to high platform status are shown.

0500-0539	Pullman	1923	4/Wh. #514E	44,500	in service	7, 24
0540-0547	Pullman	1924	4/Wh. #514E	44,500	in service	7
0548-0587	St. Louis	1951	4/Wh. #1432H	47,700	in service	7, 22

NOTES

(1) Cars 01-0150 built as open-platform cars, but later converted to closed vestibules. Boston open-platform cars were unusual in that motorman's station was located in a glassed-in booth on the front platform of lead car.

(2) First cars built with closed vestibules.

(3) First all-steel cars; cars 01 through 0174 were wooden vehicles, while 0175-0219 were built with steel frames, steel bodies below the letterboards, and wooden roofs.

(4) First deck-roof cars, a feature continued on all subsequent orders through 01000.

(5) Following cars still in service on the M.B.T.A. as work equipment: 0210, 0987, 0986, 0996, 0997, 01000.

(6) The 01100 s are 55 feet long; all previous el equipment was approximately 46 feet long, with minor variations between different classes of cars.

(7) Semi-permanently coupled in two car sets, with motorman's cab at one end of each car only.

(8) All cars in 0600-0754 fleet featured "fish belly" side sills, except 0640-0659.

(9) All cars in 0600-0754 fleet built with longitudinal seating. In 1947, after creation of the M.T.A., cars 0706, 0719, 0720 and 0724 were reconditioned with upholstered transverse seating, fluorescent lighting, "Railvane" fans and other modern appointments. They were called the "Braintree cars," since M.T.A. was attempting to develop interest in extending Dorchester line to that community.

(10) Car 0719 (cf. note 9) preserved at Seashore Trolley Museum in Kennebunkport, Maine. In addition following cars are retained by M.B.T.A. for work service: 0709, 0749, 0753 and 0754.

(11) Cars 01490 and 01491 built with experimental one piece fiberglass end; builder Pullman-Standard was anxious to test technique before using it on an entire order of cars for Chicago Transit Authority.

(12) Cars feature full width transverse cab at control end; 01400's and 01600's, since coupled into two car sets, have but a single cab per car, while single unit 01500's have two cabs each.

(13) Brushed aluminum exterior and fully air conditioned.

(14) Car 6270 preserved at Seashore Trolley Museum in Kennebunkport, Maine. Center-entrance cars 6131 and 6309 retained by M.B.T.A. for work service.

(15) Car 3001 only Boston P.C.C. not equipped with left-hand door for subway service.

(16) Cars delivered without multiple-unit controls; after opening of Riverside Line in 1959, m.u. wiring installed at Everett Shops in entire class, except car 3010, which was scrapped after a 1954 accident.

(17) This is only series of standard war-time P.C.C. s delivered from Pullman equipped with a roof monitor and forced air ventilation. Subsequently many additional P.C.C. s were so equipped, and on a random basis; "all electric" cars 3197-3221 and "picture window" cars 3271-3321 also came with "factory installed" roof monitors.

(18) All Boston P.C.C. s are air-electric cars except this series, which is "all electric." These cars not equipped with m.u. controls when built, but were upgraded to m.u. status in 1960. They do not train with air-electric cars.

(19) "All electric" and "picture window" cars are only P.C.C. s with standee windows.

(20) Double-ended cars purchased second hand from Dallas Railway and Terminal Company in 1958- 59. Most assigned to Mattapan-Ashmont Line, but several operate tripper service between Park Street and Northeastern University on Huntington Avenue Line.

(21) Ex-Dallas cars currently only P.C.C. s that do not feature m.u. controls. All other Boston P.C.C. s are m.u. equipped, although as has been noted, two classes did not arrive from builder with this feature. Original P.C.C. 3001 was not m.u.

(22) Only high platform cars in Boston featuring but two doors per side; also only cars currently in passenger service not built by Pullman-Standard.

(23) Because each car of a two car set has different electrical gear aboard, cars have different weights. So-called "A" car weighs 62,976 pounds, while "B" car weighs 61,570 pounds.

(24) Cars 0500-0587 equipped with third rail shoes and pantographs.

(25) Not equipped with m.u. connections.

(26) This series known as "picture window" cars, the only domestic P.C.C. s so built.

(27) Nos. 6000-6404, 7000-7224 are center-entrance cars.

(28) Nos. 3001-3346 are P.C.C. cars.

(Photos from M.B.T.A.)

60

YARDS AND SHOPS

Equipment Storage Yards[1]

Green Line:	Riverside	Red Line:	Harvard (Eliot)
	Boston College		Ashmont (Codman)
	Reservoir		Mattapan[2]
	Arborway	Orange Line:	Sullivan Square
Blue Line:	Orient Heights		Forest Hills[6]

Maintenance and Repair Facilities[5]

Green Line:	Reservoir	Red Line:	Harvard (Eliot)[7]
	Watertown[3]	Orange Line:	Forest Hills[6]
	Arborway		Sullivan Square
	Everett[4]		Everett
Blue Line:	Orient Heights		

NOTES

(1) Excluded from this listing are several locations where storage *tracks* can be found. Only formal storage *yards* are included.

(2) Facility for P.C.C. cars operating on Mattapan-Ashmont Line.

(3) Trolley service has not been operated on Watertown Line since June of 1969, but tracks and wire remain in place, and the car barn at Watertown is used to repair Green Line equipment.

(4) There is no longer a track connection between Everett and the Green Line network. Cars must be hauled to Everett aboard a flat-bed trailer rig from a ramp at Lechmere Terminal. The same procedure is used when equipment must be transferred to the Mattapan-Ashmont Line.

(5) Funds are now available for two new maintenance facilities. A car barn is scheduled to be built at Riverside to ease pressure on the aging Reservoir installation. And the South Bay Maintenance Center is being built on the site of the New Haven Railroad's Dover Street Yards in South Boston to serve the Red Line. Once completed, the M.B.T.A. will abandon Eliot Shops and Yard, and the John F. Kennedy Memorial Library will then be built on the site.

(6) Storage facilities for the Main Line Elevated were previously located at ground level just north of the Forest Hills station. Additionally a shop and storage yard was located at Guild Street, just south of Dudley Station. This was closed in 1923 when the Forest Hills facility was opened.

(7) Between 1954 and 1971, trolley cars on the Mattapan-Ashmont shuttle were maintained at Eliot Shops. When in need of service they would be towed from Dorchester to Cambridge behind a conventional train. Construction of a small repair barn at Mattapan has eliminated this practice; Everett Shops also remain available for shuttle cars (cf. note 4).

POWER AND SIGNALS

All Boston subways, els and trolleys operate on 600 volts of direct current. This electricity is generated in company-owned plants, and transmitted throughout the system by a complex network of cables and feeders. When the West End Street Ry first turned to electricity in 1889, it was presumed that direct current could be generated in the plants as such; large installations were built to do just that. One of them, the Lincoln Wharf Station, is shown at left in an early view complete with Atlantic Avenue El tracks and horse transportation underneath. Later it was discovered that a more efficient method was to generate electricity as alternating current, which has better transmission qualities than d.c., and convert the a.c. to d.c. only at substations located through the system. By 1931 the last of the d.c. generators had been phased out.

The M.B.T.A. still generates most of its own electricity, which is something of a rarity in the urban transit industry today. An advantage of this policy was emphasized during the famous Northeast Blackout of 1965. Whereas New York's subways ground to a halt, the M.B.T.A. gave full service through the entire outage.

On page 60, the three-indication signal with its innards displayed for the photographer shows the basic tool that has long protected riders of Boston's subways and rapid transit lines. The new South Shore Line employs an advance system by which signals are transmitted to the train and displayed on a console in the cab.

When M.B.T.A. was created in 1964, it adopted a colorless grey paint scheme for the P.C.C. fleet, though few cars ever were painted to specifications. In 1971, an attractive grey, white and green pattern was unveiled. Here No. 3250 prepares to depart from Lechmere, smartly enameled in the new design. (Tom Nelligan photo)

COLOR CODING, THEN AND NOW

A quotation taken from: *History of the West End Street Railway* Boston: Louis P. Hager, 1892, p. 26:

In order to make the routes of the various cars understood, a system of painting was adopted, which was calculated to aid those who patronized the various lines, so that, even at a distance, they might be easily and readily recognized and all mistakes avoided. This system will undoubtedly be maintained after all the lines are operating by electricity. The colors adopted are as follows:

The cars on the Mount Pleasant line and all those running to Meetinghouse Hill, or to Dorchester avenue and Fields Corner, are ultramarine blue, ornamented with gilt.

Cars of the Warren street lines, Egleston square, to Norfolk House, to East Boston Ferry on Washington street, Hampden street, Roxbury and Charlestown, rapid transit Warren Street via Harrison avenue to Post Office Square, and Atlantic avenue on Washington street, are green, with gilt letters.

Huntington avenue line, Dartmouth street, West Chester park to Boston & Maine, Fitchburg, Eastern and Lowell railroad stations, and Back Bay cars are a peacock blue.

Cars to and from Jamaica Plain, East Boston and Chelsea ferry on Tremont street, Lenox street, Columbus avenue and Atlantic avenue on Tremont street, are yellow.

On all the Charlestown lines the cars are painted a buff with gilt letters.

All cars from and to Cambridge are carmine.

All K street, City Point, Bay View and other South Boston cars are vermilion.

Signs are displayed on all cars showing their direction, so that passengers can readily determine whether they are going to or coming from the point they desire to reach.

A quotation taken from: *Design in Transit* Boston: The Institute of Contemporary Art, 1967, p. 3:

After a thorough reconnaissance of the system, Cambridge Seven Associates presented plans for its redesign. To make clear the structure of the transit system as they saw it, they designed maps in which color was a key element. The Authority's four major lines were renamed: Red (Cambridge-Dorchester), Orange (Main Line Elevated), Green (the Boylston-Tremont trolley subway), and Blue (East Boston). Information related to each line was also to be printed in its own color, so that a hurried traveler need only follow the color coding.

Not generally identified with the subway but a most interesting BE Ry street car development was this articulated unit, sometimes referred to as "two rooms and a bath." Cars of series 0175 and 0220 appear in a four-car train at rest on Main Line El structure in upper background. (M.B.T.A.)

CENTER-ENTRANCE CAR PROTOTYPE

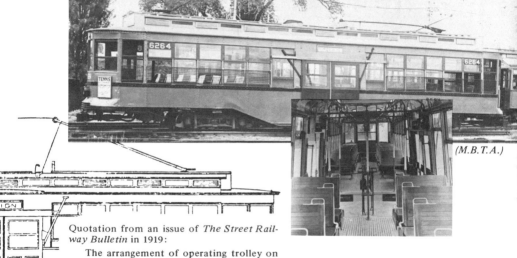

(M.B.T.A.)

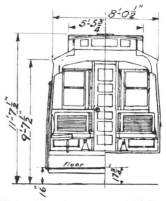

Quotation from an issue of *The Street Railway Bulletin* in 1919:

The arrangement of operating trolley on these cars differs from that in general use on standard double-end cars, in that the forward trolley pole is used instead of the rear. This is made possible by an ingenious arrangement which consists of a trap or opening extending crosswise of car between monitor frames. This is fitted with a hinged cover which is flanged all around for the exclusion of water and which is operated from within the car.

The trolley cord passes down through a small opening in this trap to the trolley catcher which is located on a cross pipe at stanchion at edges of low level floor. If the trolley leaves the wire, it is only necessary for the conductor to open the trap and replace the trolley, which he does without opening the doors and leaving the car unprotected . . . . The length of the trap permits the replacing of trolley on the sharpest curves.

(Additional drawings on page 64 following)

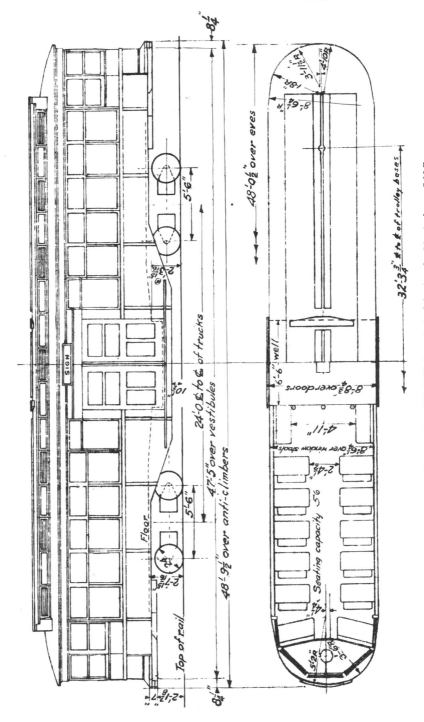

BE Ry blueprints for cars No. 6000-6049. Laconia Arch-bar trucks. Westinghouse S.M.E. brake. GE PC-5-A control. Date:1/5/17. Reduced to HO scale. (Courtesy of M.B.T.A.)

388.42   Cudahy **760210**
C   Change at Park
                  Street Under
                            4.95

FEB 23 2000

FINES - 5c PER DAY
       10¢

The Public Library of New London

New London, Connecticut 06320

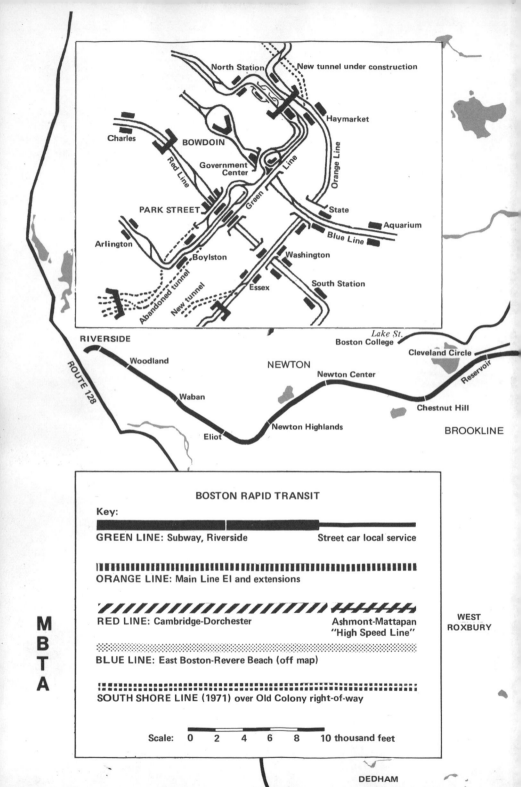

BOSTON RAPID TRANSIT

Key:

GREEN LINE: Subway, Riverside   Street car local service

ORANGE LINE: Main Line El and extensions

RED LINE: Cambridge-Dorchester   Ashmont-Mattapan "High Speed Line"

BLUE LINE: East Boston-Revere Beach (off map)

SOUTH SHORE LINE (1971) over Old Colony right-of-way

Scale: 0   2   4   6   8   10 thousand feet